"And now a tale of friendship and flatulence in the last place you would expect to find either. I present..."

The Drunk in the Trunk

By Dr. Brews

You went out for a burger
at a great local bar,

When a hammered old man...

...took a nap in your car.

You drove home and never noticed him way in the back,

By the spare tire, tools, jumper cables and jack.

Now you pull into the driveway and
suddenly hear,
A muffled aged voice ask...

You detect a stench— not unlike a skunk,
And then you find him...

...The Drunk in the Trunk!

He staggers inside with a hiccup
and heave,

Then raids your liquor and
refuses to leave!

When you get to know him—
he's not all that bad,

But when you run out of whiskey,
he tends to get mad.

Sure he smells bad and drops the occasional fart,

But he's a fun-loving guy with a really big heart.

He's warm...

...and he's kind...

...and he never steals,

He just wants beer and whiskey for all three meals!

He's hopelessly messy and
shamelessly gassy,
Yet get past the fumes...

...and he's surprisingly classy.

So whenever you're down or your day's filled with strife,

Call the drunk in the trunk. He's
your friend for life.

The End.

"How about that ending? Learn from
life, friends– – and drink up!"
Until next time, cheers."

Jackanapes Studios LLC
IMMATURE CONTENT FOR IMMATURE PEOPLE.

JACKANAPES@JACKANAPESSTUDIOS.COM

FOLLOW US ON:
INSTAGRAM @ JACKANAPESSTUDIOS
X @ JACKANAPESSTDS

Coming Soon...
The Wino on the Rhino